Teresa E. Hearn

Business Conversation for All

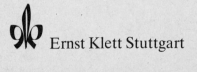 Ernst Klett Stuttgart

1. Auflage   1 6 5 4 3 | 1985 84 83 82

Alle Drucke dieser Auflage können im Unterricht nebeneinander benutzt werden. Die letzte Zahl bezeichnet das Jahr dieses Druckes. © Ernst Klett, Stuttgart 1978. Nach dem Urheberrechtsgesetz vom 9. Sept. 1965 i.d.F. vom 10. Nov. 1972 ist die Vervielfältigung oder Übertragung urheberrechtlich geschützter Werke, also auch der Texte, Illustrationen und Graphiken dieses Buches, nicht gestattet. Dieses Verbot erstreckt sich auch auf die Vervielfältigung für Zwecke der Unterrichtsgestaltung – mit Ausnahme der in den §§ 53, 54 URG ausdrücklich genannten Sonderfälle –, wenn nicht die Einwilligung des Verlages vorher eingeholt wurde. Im Einzelfall muß über die Zahlung einer Gebühr für die Nutzung fremden geistigen Eigentums entschieden werden. Als Vervielfältigung gelten alle Verfahren einschließlich der Fotokopie, der Übertragung auf Matrizen, der Speicherung auf Bändern, Platten, Transparenten oder anderen Medien.

Cartoons: Syndication International, London.

Umschlaggestaltung: Zembsch' Werkstatt, München.

Druck: Eugen Gloß, Stuttgart. Printed in Germany.

ISBN 3-12-514120-6

Vorwort

"Business Conversation for All" wendet sich an alle, die beabsichtigen, ihre Grundkenntnisse des Englischen zu festigen, weiterzuentwickeln und zu verfeinern. Die Dialoge, die um die wichtigsten allgemeinen wirtschaftlichen bzw. geschäftlichen Themen kreisen, verhelfen dem Lernenden zu flüssigem und mühelosen Gebrauch wirtschaftssprachlicher Wörter und Wendungen.

Die folgende Methode hat sich bei der Arbeit mit diesem Buch bewährt: Den Kursteilnehmern wird der Dialog zunächst bei geschlossenen Büchern von Band oder Schallplatte vorgespielt oder er wird mit verteilten Rollen vorgelesen. Die Kursteilnehmer haben dann Gelegenheit, unbekannte oder schwierige Wörter und Ausdrücke zu klären, bevor der Dialog bei geöffneten Büchern wiederholt wird. Dann sollten die Fragen zum Textverständnis – mündlich oder schriftlich – beantwortet werden.

Wiederholtes Hören und Sprechen der Dialogszenen dient dazu, sich das der jeweiligen Situation angemessene Englisch einzuprägen mit dem Ziel, selbst auf englisch Geschäftsgespräche zu führen.

Die Lösungsvorschläge zu den Verständnisfragen und eine Zusammenstellung der gebräuchlichsten Sätze und Redewendungen zu typischen Gesprächssituationen im Anhang machen das Buch in Verbindung mit den Schallplatten (Klettnummer 51411), der Compact-Cassette (Klettnummer 51417) oder dem Tonband (Klettnummer 51418) auch für den Selbstunterricht zu einem geeigneten Instrument, authentisches wirtschaftssprachliches Englisch zu erwerben.

Contents

On the telephone – Inquiries – Quotations and offers –
Orders – Packing and dispatch – Accounts and payment –
Complaints – Replies to complaints – Insurance – Travel
arrangements – Agencies – Applying for a job

1. Final arrangements

A group of German data-programmers are coming over to their firm's head office in England for a training course. A few days before they are due to arrive, Herr Bauer, who is the staff manager for the German branch of the firm, phones up to make sure that everything is in order.

Mr Spencer: Spencer here.

Herr Bauer: Good morning, Mr Spencer. This is Mr Bauer from Frankfurt.

Mr Spencer: Ah, good morning, Mr Bauer. I was expecting you to phone.

Herr Bauer: Yes, I phoned earlier, but the girl I spoke to said you were out.

Mr Spencer: That was my secretary. She passed on the message you left, though. I understand that you want to discuss the arrangements for the course that some of your people are attending here.

Herr Bauer: That's right. Firstly, only eight of the thirteen who we originally registered will be coming. The other five have had to cancel for various reasons.

Mr Spencer: I see. And when will they be arriving?

Herr Bauer: Their plane is due to arrive at Heathrow at 4.49 on Tuesday evening, that is May 14th. Has accommodation been arranged for them?

Mr Spencer: Yes, we've reserved single rooms with baths at the George Hotel here in Croydon for the whole time, 17 days to be exact, up to and including May 30th.

Herr Bauer: Ah yes, that's the hotel which the last group stayed at. That'll be fine.

Mr Spencer: I assume that they will be flying back the evening that the course finishes.

Herr Bauer: Yes. Except for one, who wants to stay another week, they are all booked on the 20.45 flight from Heathrow.

Mr Spencer: Good, we'll arrange for them to be taken to the airport in time then. By the way, have they received the information sheets which we sent out last week?

Herr Bauer: Yes. I must say, it looks the most interesting course that we've had yet.

Mr Spencer: Well, we've certainly done our best to make it so. We've learnt a lot from the last one that we held.

Herr Bauer: Right, I think that's everything I wanted to ask. I hope it all goes off well.

Mr Spencer: Thank you. We'll look forward to seeing the group on Tuesday then. Good-bye.

Annotations

to assume to take as true

Comprehension Questions

1. What is Mr Bauer phoning up to discuss?
2. When and where will the group be arriving?
3. What arrangements have been made for their accommodation?
4. When will they be flying back? What flight are they booked on?
5. What does Mr Spencer ask about the information sheets?
6. What does Mr Bauer say about the course?

2. Mixing business with pleasure

Herr Hansen, the export manager of a German firm which has developed a device to reduce air pollution by cars, is visiting Mr Evans, the manager of a large English car manufacturing firm, to whom he hopes to sell it. They are discussing the matter over lunch.

Herr Hansen: This is a very pleasant restaurant.

Mr Evans: Yes, I've been coming here for years. It's become rather expensive though, but eating is an expensive business anywhere in London these days.

Herr Hansen: It's certainly worth knowing about a place like this. The food is excellent.

Mr Evans: Yes. It's a shame to have to spoil it by talking business.

Herr Hansen: Yes, isn't it?

Mr Evans: Now, as I understand from what you've been saying, this device that your firm has developed can be fitted to any car, and will reduce pollution by up to 70 per cent.

Herr Hansen: Yes, that's right.

Mr Evans: Am I not right in thinking that the Americans recently produced something very similar?

Herr Hansen: Cleanfilter, you mean? Yes and no. Their device is similar in so far as it performs the same function. There are, however, quite basic differences.

Mr Evans: At any rate there is no danger of our getting into difficulties with the patent office?

Herr Hansen: None at all. Moreover, our device has the advantage of being considerably cheaper than the American one, owing to lower production costs and the lower import charges within the Common Market.

Mr Evans: This all sounds very interesting. I shall, of course, have to discuss the matter with our managing director before making any decision.

Herr Hansen: Yes, of course.

Mr Evans: I should also like a more detailed explanation as to exactly how the device works. But I think you can look forward to receiving a positive answer within the next week.

Herr Hansen: I'm very pleased to hear it.

Mr Evans: And now how about a Cognac to finish off the meal?

Herr Hansen: That's an excellent idea.

Comprehension Questions

1. Who are Herr Hansen and Mr Evans?
2. What are they meeting to discuss?
3. What does Mr Evans say about eating in London?
4. What will the German firm's device do?
5. Why is Mr Evans worried that they might get into trouble with the patent office? Why, according to Herr Hansen, is there no danger of this?
6. What advantage has the German device over the American one? What are the reasons for this?

3. At an exhibition stand

An English buyer is attending an International Exhibition of Office Furniture and Equipment in Geneva. He is very interested in the display on the stand of a Swiss firm, and approaches the girl on the stand:

Buyer: Good morning. I'm a buyer for Carter and Jones, dealers in office furniture and equipment. You've probably heard of us.

Representative: Carter and Jones? Yes, of course I have. You must be the largest firm in that line in Great Britain.

Buyer: Well, we're always on the look out for new ideas, and my attention was caught by that desk and chair over there.

Representative: They're models from our latest range. It's not even in production yet, but it's already won two design awards.

Buyer: I certainly haven't seen such an interesting design for a long time. Could you tell me more about it?

Representative: Certainly. Firstly, the cushions of the chair are fastened by a special tape, and are changeable. The chair itself can be adjusted.

Buyer: That can sometimes be quite a complicated business.

Representative: Not on this model. Unlike most chairs, this one can easily be adjusted with the person sitting on it.

Buyer: That's an advantage.

Representative: The height and the back rest can be moved to exactly the right position, which is essential for office workers who spend so great a part of the day sitting down.

Buyer: Yes, that I can understand. And how about the

desk? I rather like the colour scheme. It's not often you see such cheerful colours in an office.

Representative: This desk can be had with a number of variations, as well as in any of 6 modern colours, as you can see in our new catalogue.

Buyer: And I can see from the catalogue that there is sufficient drawer space for papers, files, etc.

Representative: Yes, the system has been so designed that everything one needs – papers, files, telephone, dictating machine etc. – can be kept within easy reach.

Buyer: I must say, it looks very well planned.

Representative: Would you be interested in a visit to our showrooms in Zürich?

Buyer: I'm afraid I shan't have time. I'll study your catalogue over lunch and come back sometime during the afternoon to place my order.

Representative: I'll look forward to seeing you this afternoon, then.

Annotations

on the look out for watching out for – **award** prize – **design** [di'zain] *here:* Ausführung – **to adjust** [əd'ʒʌst] to alter s.th. in order to make it suitable for use – **scheme** [ski:m] – **variation** [ˌvɛəri'eiʃən] slight difference – **to design** *here:* konstruieren

Comprehension Questions

1. What sort of a firm is Carter and Jones?
2. What does the representative tell the buyer about the chair?
3. Why is it so essential that one should be able to adjust the height and back rest of an office chair to exactly the right position?
4. What does the buyer like about the desk? Why does he find it unusual?
5. How has the furniture system been designed?
6. What does the buyer intend to do when he leaves the stand?

4. Life on strike

In spite of the government pay freeze, the electricity workers are on strike for more pay. Two of them meet one evening in a pub and discuss the situation.

Frank: Hello, Bill! How's life?

Bill: Not so bad, under the circumstances, Frank. I'm glad to be out of the house, though.

Frank: Why's that?

Bill: My wife's done nothing but complain all day.

Frank: What about?

Bill: She said if I didn't go back to work within the next week she'd leave me and go to her mother's. She thinks we're being irresponsible in trying to breach the pay freeze.

Frank: What does she mean by that?

Bill: She argues that everyone's in the same boat, and that by striking we're only helping the country on its way to economic ruin, instead of building it up.

Frank: That's all very well, but we were promised a year ago that our pay situation would be reviewed annually to keep pace with inflationary trends. That promise has not been kept, so we must fight for it.

Bill: I heard on the news this evening that half the factories in the Midlands had been forced to stop production because of their dependence on electricity. 20,000 men had been sent home.

Frank: Good. That shows we're having an effect.

Bill: Ford claim that the strike has already wiped out their profit for the whole of this year.

Frank: That's exactly why we must stay firm. If we give in now we'll have gained nothing.

Bill: How are the negotiations going, by the way? Have you heard?

Frank: I met Tom Hancock just now, and he said it was deadlock. Neither the Union nor the employers will give an inch.

Bill: Well, let's hope they come to a settlement soon.

Frank: Yes. Will you have another pint, Bill?

Bill: No, thanks. My wife asked me not to stay too long – we've got visitors coming this evening.

Frank: Well, cheerio, then. See you tomorrow.

Bill: Yes, cheerio.

Annotations

pay freeze government measure by which no pay increases are allowed – **irresponsible** opposite of responsible – **to breach** to break through – **to review** *here:* to re-examine and change – **dependence** [–'––] state of depending on s.th. – **deadlock** ['––] complete failure to reach an agreement – **not to give an inch** not to give in at all – **settlement** agreement

Comprehension Questions

1. Why is Bill glad to be out of the house?
2. Why does Bill's wife think that the electricity workers are being irresponsible in trying to breach the pay freeze?
3. How does Frank justify the strike?
4. What effect has the strike had on industry in the Midlands?
5. What is Frank's reaction to the effect of the strike on industry?
6. What progress is being made in the negotiations? Why is this so?
7. Do you think the electricity workers are right to stand firm, or do you think they are being irresponsible?

5. To smoke or not to smoke

A television interview

Interviewer: This week the dangers of cigarette smoking have been brought into the public eye again through the campaign which was begun by the British Cancer Society on Saturday. Today we have invited Mr McBride, the Chairman of the Society, to tell us about the campaign. Firstly, Mr McBride, what do you hope to achieve by it?

Mr McBride: As we said in our statement at the beginning of the campaign, we hope to make the public aware that cigarette smoking harms the health.

Interviewer: How do you hope to do this?

Mr McBride: We've sent out over two million leaflets, we've had posters printed, and we've managed to acquire free advertising space in many papers and magazines, as well as time on radio and television.

Interviewer: When the managing director of United Tobacco was asked recently how he felt about this campaign, he said: "I'm not too concerned. The British Cancer Society held a similar campaign last year, which didn't do the industry any harm." What do you say to that?

Mr McBride: It's true that last year's campaign was not a great success, but we are confident of achieving much better results this time.

Interviewer: He also claimed that the tobacco companies are already doing enough. They have put a warning on cigarette packets, advertising has been barred from television, and last year United Tobacco contributed £50,000 to Cancer Research, and have planned to increase it to £100,000 this year.

Mr McBride: The main aim of the cigarette industry, however, is to sell more and more cigarettes, which are harmful to the health.

Interviewer: Are there any figures to support this statement?

Mr McBride: Well, two investigations, one which British doctors held in 1959, and the American Terry report of 1964, revealed some alarming facts.

Interviewer: Can you give us an example of these facts?

Mr McBride: Well, both investigations found that the death rate of smokers aged between 35 and 70 was more than a third higher than that of non-smokers in the same age group.

Interviewer: As high as that?

Mr McBride: Yes, and the rate was a hundred per cent higher for 50 to 70-year-olds. The main cause for this higher rate was heart disease.

Interviewer: That certainly is alarming. Unfortunately, though, we shall have to leave the discussion there for today as our time has run out. Thank you for coming along, Mr McBride.

Annotations

concerned worried – **to reveal** [ri'vi:l] to uncover, bring to light

Comprehension Questions

1. What does the British Cancer Society hope to achieve by its campaign?
2. What has the society done so far to publicize the campaign?
3. Why wasn't the managing director of United Tobacco concerned about the campaign?
4. What do the tobacco companies already do which the managing director considers is enough?
5. How do the aims of the British Cancer Society and those of the tobacco companies differ?

14

6. The missing money

A telephone conversation with the Bank Manager

Mr Finney: May I speak to Mr Bell, please?

Telephonist: Would you hold the line, please? I'll connect you …

Mr Bell: Bell here.

Mr Finney: Good morning, Mr Bell. This is Mr Finney.

Mr Bell: Good morning, Mr Finney. What can I do for you?

Mr Finney: This morning I received a letter informing me that my account was overdrawn. That can't possibly be true. I've kept a strict record of my expenses, and I should have £212.

Mr Bell: If you'll hold the line a minute I'll see if I can find out what's happened …

… Hello, Mr Finney?

Mr Finney: Yes?

Mr Bell: I'm sorry to have kept you waiting. You're Mr Charles Robert Finney, is that right?

Mr Finney: Yes, that's right.

Mr Bell: Well, according to our records, nothing has been paid into your account for the last three months, and you do in fact have an overdraft of £128.

Mr Finney: There must be some mistake. My firm assures me that my salary has been paid in every month as usual.

Mr Bell: Then the mistake must be at our end. As you know, we changed over to a computer system three months ago, and as is inevitable in the early stages of any new system, there have been a few teething troubles.

Mr Finney: Do you think you will be able to find the mistake?

Mr Bell: Oh yes, it is probably due to a slight error in programming which can be corrected quite easily.

Mr Finney: That's a relief.

Mr Bell: If you could ring back in two or three days' time we should have been able to trace the error by then.

Mr Finney: All right. I'll do that, then. Good-bye.

Mr Bell: Good-bye, Mr Finney.

Annotations

to overdraw an account to draw more money (from the bank) than one has on one's account – **inevitable** [–´– – – –] unable to be avoided – **teething troubles** difficulties appearing at the beginning of a new system etc. and not likely to last

Comprehension Questions

1. What information does the letter contain which Mr Finney received from the bank? Why does he think it can't be true?
2. What, according to the bank's records, is the situation regarding Mr Finney's account?
3. Why does Mr Finney think there must be some mistake?
4. Why doesn't Mr Bell seem surprised that the mistake is probably at their end?
5. What does Mr Bell think must have happened?

7. Computerised Export Intelligence

Mr Fox, the export manager of an electrical appliance firm, reads an advertisement for Computerised Export Intelligence. He is interested in the scheme and rings their number.

Telephonist: Computerised Export Intelligence. Can I help you?

Mr Fox: Extension 7122, please …

Mr Benson: Benson here.

Mr Fox: This is Mr Fox, of Brown and Harris Ltd., manufacturers of electrical appliances. I read your advertisement in the *Financial Times* today and wondered if you could give me further information.

Mr Benson: Certainly. What would you like to know?

Mr Fox: In what ways could your service be of help to a small firm such as ours?

Mr Benson: In many ways, Mr Fox. In fact it is especially helpful for smaller firms which haven't the facilities for market research that larger firms have.

Mr Fox: What form would this help take?

Mr Benson: From our Commercial Diplomatic posts in many countries abroad we receive regular reports on all aspects of industry and commerce. From these we could pass on to you any information that could be valuable to you.

Mr Fox: What sort of information, for instance?

Mr Benson: Well, you could choose the type of information you wanted from the very wide selection we offer. For example, of specific interest to your firm would probably be notification of the changes in tariff and import regulations overseas.

Mr Fox: Yes, that would be a help.

Mr Benson: Overnight you would receive from us information on potential markets it could take you weeks, months or even years to accumulate on your own.

Mr Fox: That would save a lot of time and trouble. And the £25 subscription would cover everything – the service, the literature and the postage?

Mr Benson: Yes, it would. Would you like our representative to call on you and discuss how the service can best serve your requirements?

Mr Fox: Yes, I would.

Mr Benson: Then if you give me your telephone number, I'll get him to contact you.

Annotations

potential [pəu'tenʃəl] possible in the future – **literature** ['litritʃə] *here:* written matter on a subject – **to get s.o. to do s.th.** to ask, persuade s.o. to do s.th.

Comprehension Questions

1. How did Mr Fox hear about Computerised Export Intelligence?
2. Why is a service such as Computerised Export Intelligence especially useful to smaller firms?
3. Where does Computerised Export Intelligence get its information from?
4. What sort of information can it pass on to firms?
5. How much is the subscription? What does it cover?

8. Starting up in Brazil

A British firm of engine manufacturers is hoping to be given an order to supply the Brazilian airline with 20 engines. The managing director and the financial director discuss the situation.

Managing Director: I've just heard from Brazil. They want someone to go over there to talk about this order. I thought you and I could go at the beginning of next week.

Financial Director: Good idea. What's the position at the moment? We aren't the only ones to have been approached, are we?

Managing Director: No, we've got competition from a French firm and an Italian one. But we hope to be the first to negotiate.

Financial Director: It would be a good thing for the company to win the order.

Managing Director: Yes, we've been trying to get into South America for a long time.

Financial Director: Do you think we're likely to be able to expand once we're there?

Managing Director: It's hard to say. It's only one order, of course, but the first is usually the hardest. What we are going to investigate, though, is the possibility of setting up a factory in Brazil.

Financial Director: Yes, I should think that would be a lot more economical in the long run. What's the position for foreign companies wanting to start up in Brazil?

Managing Director: It seems to be ideal. They're encouraging foreign investment of all kinds, and there are practically no restrictions.

Financial Director: What are the sales prospects? I mean, it's no good our being able to produce the goods cheaply if we can't sell them.

Managing Director: They're supposed to be very good, but that will have to be investigated, too.

Financial Director: At least the Brazilian economy looks healthy – it's expanding at an astonishing rate.

Managing Director: Yes, but it's impossible to say how long that will last. We won't really know what to do for the best until we have all the facts in front of us.

Financial Director: And a visit to Brazil behind us. That's one part of the business I really am looking forward to.

Managing Director: Yes. Perhaps we can make it last a couple of weeks to make it really worthwhile.

Comprehension Questions

1. Is the British firm the only one to have been approached by the Brazilian airline?
2. Why would it be particularly good for the company to win the order?
3. What possibility is the firm going to investigate?
4. What is Brazil's attitude to foreign investment?
5. What is the situation regarding the Brazilian economy?

9. A new idea in shirts

A British firm has produced throw-away shirts for men, but before marketing them, they get a marketing consultant to test public reaction. The marketing manager and the marketing consultant meet to discuss the results of the test.

Manager: Well, Mr Hornby, what's your general impression?

Consultant: It's hard to say. Wait until you know the details and then you can judge for yourself.

Manager: Good. Can you first tell me something about the project?

Consultant: Certainly. 70,000 shirts were distributed in all – 7 each, that is a week's supply, to 10,000 men, or rather homes.

Manager: Why do you say that?

Consultant: Because in this project the women are as important as the men.

Manager: In what way?

Consultant: Well, it's the men who wear the shirts, but women usually have quite a bit of influence on what is worn by their husbands.

Manager: Yes, I know what you mean. Go on.

Consultant: They were asked to try them out for a week and to answer a few questions when our rep. called back.

Manager: And how did people react?

Consultant: Some didn't like the idea of being experimented on, but most people were persuaded to take part in the end.

Manager: What did they think of the idea of throw-away shirts?

Consultant: As was to be expected, most of the women said they thought they were a good idea.

Manager: That's encouraging.

Consultant: Yes, but the men were not so convinced. Although 32 per cent thought they were a good idea in principle, only 10 per cent would want to wear them themselves.

Manager: What reasons were given by the other 90 per cent for not wanting to wear them?

Consultant: They varied, but they all pointed to a general mistrust.

Manager: What do you mean?

Consultant: Well, Englishmen are on the whole very conservative about their clothes. They are not easily won over to new ideas and materials.

Manager: Yes, I was afraid of that.

Consultant: They might be persuaded to change their minds with enough advertising propaganda, though.

Manager: How would you advise us to go about it?

Consultant: Your advertising should be aimed at the businessman who has to travel and attend meetings, and needs to change his shirts frequently – and the wife of such a man, of course.

Manager: Good. I'll look at the exact figures carefully, and discuss them and what you've told me with the sales manager and the managing director. Thank you, Mr Hornby, I'll let you know what we decide.

Annotations

rep. representative – **mistrust** ['–'–] lack of trust

Comprehension Questions

1. How many men took part in the market research project?
2. Why were the women as important as the men in this project?
3. What did the women think of the throw-away shirts?
4. How many of the men would be prepared to wear them themselves? What reason does the consultant give for so many not wanting to wear them?
5. What does the consultant advise the firm to do?
6. Do you think throw-away clothing is a good idea? Say why or why not.

10. The wonders of the computer

Mr Johnson, the manager of a mail-order firm has invited Mr Dennis, a representative of a computer firm, to come and discuss the possibilities of his firm going over to a computer system.

Mr Johnson: How would a computer improve our system?

Mr Dennis: In several ways, Mr Johnson. However efficient a manual system is, it is unavoidably inaccurate and slow.

Mr Johnson: But computers are complicated things. Don't they make just as many mistakes?

Mr Dennis: Computers don't make mistakes, except when they really break down. They are usually just wrongly programmed, but these mistakes can easily be corrected.

Mr Johnson: What would a computer be able to do in an organization like ours?

Mr Dennis: Well, I'd have to look at the whole system more closely before I could tell you exactly, but there are already various programs in existence which could be used.

Mr Johnson: From your experience with other firms, can you give me a rough idea of what could be expected?

Mr Dennis: Certainly. You would probably need a central computer, in which would be stored all the facts about the stores situation and the customers – their names, addresses and reference numbers, of course, and the details of their accounts.

Mr Johnson: These facts are constantly changing. Could they easily be kept up to date?

Mr Dennis: Quite easily. When the facts change, the computer automatically changes its records.

Mr Johnson: Does it work in the same way for customers' accounts?

Mr Dennis: Yes, when a customer places an order or makes a payment, his account is altered accordingly. And if his regular payments are overdue, the computer will automatically print out a reminder.

Mr Johnson: If I want a permanent record of a situation, is that possible?

Mr Dennis: Quite possible. At regular intervals – weekly or monthly, perhaps – you can have a printout, that is a printed record, of anything you want – the stores situation, customers' accounts, etc.

Mr Johnson: Such a computer must be pretty expensive.

Mr Dennis: The initial outlay is not small. But labour is costly, and so are errors, and what you save in labour costs and gain in efficiency would make it a really worthwhile investment.

Mr Johnson: Thank you, Mr Dennis. It sounds quite promising.

Annotations

manual ['mænjuəl] done with the hands – **printout** ['– –] printed information from the computer – **outlay** ['– –] sum of money that is spent – **costly** expensive

Comprehension Questions

1. What does Mr Dennis say about manual systems?
2. What is the usual reason for computers making mistakes?
3. What would be stored in the central computer?
4. How would these facts be kept up to date?
5. How can a permanent record of a situation be obtained?
6. Why does Mr Dennis think that a computer would be a worthwhile investment?

11. A change of plan

Importer: I'm ringing about our order No 8973 for spare parts for the *Cleanomat 460* washing-machines.

Exporter: Yes, the order's being dealt with now. It should be ready for dispatch by Wednesday.

Importer: The problem is, in our order we asked for shipment to be by rail and sea. In the meantime, though, the spares shortage has become acute, so we need the parts urgently. Could you have them sent by air as soon as possible?

Exporter: Yes, of course. I'll get on to our dispatch department right away. By the way, you're paying by banker's transfer, aren't you?

Importer: Yes, that's right.

Exporter: Could you make it a telegraphic transfer, then?

Importer: Yes, we'll do that. And what about the shipping documents?

Exporter: We'll send them to you by airmail as soon as we have confirmation from our bank that they have received your transfer.

Importer: Good. We will, of course, be making more orders in the future. We would suggest paying for these by Documentary Letter of Credit, to be drawn at 60 days sight.

Exporter: In that case would you instruct your bank to open an Irrevocable Letter of Credit in our favour through Lloyd's Bank, Portsmouth, for the amount on the invoice.

Importer: Yes, all right. And I'll contact our bank now about the telegraphic transfer. Good-bye.

Annotations

acute [ə'kju:t] serious – **to get on to** to contact – **banker's transfer** Banküberweisung – **at (60) days sight** to be paid (60) days after receipt of draft – **Irrevocable Letter of Credit** [ˌiri'vəukəbl] unwiderrufliches Akkreditiv

Comprehension Questions

1. What is the importer ringing about?
2. How does he want the order changed? Why?
3. How was the importer paying for this order? How does the exporter want him to pay now?
4. What are the exporters going to do with the shipping documents?
5. What form of payment does the importer want to use for future orders? How does the exporter ask him to go about this?

12. A rush order

Secretary: Mr Moore – Herr Wolfgang Peters of Firma Schumann is on the line. He's phoning from Hamburg.

Mr Moore: Right, Janet, put him through. – Richard Moore here.

Herr Peters: Hello, Richard. This is Wolfgang Peters.

Mr Moore: Hello, Wolfgang, what can I do for you?

Herr Peters: That last consignment of *Masterform* shirts…

Mr Moore: Yes, I hope there was nothing wrong with them.

Herr Peters: Not at all. On the contrary, there's been an absolute rush on them. We're almost out of stock. Can you let us have 1000 more as soon as possible?

Mr Moore: Just a minute. I'll check … Yes, that's no problem. We'll dispatch them tomorrow c.i.f. Hamburg. If we can get them on the *Tilbury Star,* sailing on Wednesday, they'll arrive in Hamburg on the 28th.

Herr Peters: That'll be fine. Oh, by the way, we haven't received your winter catalogue and samples yet. Are they on the way?

"Good to get away from it all at the end of the day, isn't it?"

Mr Moore: Yes, I'm sorry about that. We've had a dispute in our dispatch department, which has held everything up. It's all sorted out now, though, and you should be getting the catalogue and samples by the end of the week.

Herr Peters: Good. Well, I think that's all for now, then. Thanks a lot. Good-bye.

Annotations

a rush on s.th. a sudden great demand for s.th. – **dispute** [dis'pju:t] argument, quarrel – **to sort out** to settle, to put right

Comprehension Questions

1. Where is Herr Peters phoning from?
2. What does he want?
3. Why is the matter so urgent?
4. How will the consignment be shipped?
5. What else does Herr Peters inquire about?
6. What reason does Mr Moore give for the delay?
7. What is the position now?

13. A wrong order

Export Manager: Thornton Ltd., John Denver speaking.

Customer: This is Marc Dupont of Mathieu et Bonnard, Paris.

Export Manager: Good afternoon, Monsieur Dupont. What can I do for you?

Customer: We've just received our order HT/498 for 25 sets of *Finlandia* cutlery. We were impressed by your prompt delivery.

Export Manager: Thank you – that's good to hear.

Customer: But when we opened the consignment we found that we'd received the wrong order. – There were only 12 sets of *Finlandia* cutlery – the other 13 sets were *Arabesque* – a line we don't usually stock.

Export Manager: Oh dear, I'm sorry about that. We've several temporary workers in the packing department at the moment, to enable us to cope with the Christmas rush, which is no doubt how the mistake came about.

Customer: Yes, I thought it was something like that. How soon can you let us have the remaining sets? It's important that we have them as soon as possible. We need them for the Christmas trade.

Export Manager: I'll get on to our dispatch department at once, and have them sent express. You should get them within the next few days.

Customer: And what do you want done with the 13 sets of *Arabesque*?

Export Manager: Would you be prepared to keep them if we grant you a 10% discount? That would be easier than sending them back, and it would save the freight and insurance costs, too.

Customer: All right, we'll do that then.

Export Manager: I apologize for the mix-up. I assure you things will be back to normal after Christmas.

Customer: Yes, of course. Well, we'll look forward to receiving the rest of the order in the near future. Good-bye.

Annotations

cutlery ['kʌtləri] knives, forks and spoons – **to impress** [–'–] to cause s.o. to think favourably of s.o. or s.th. – **prompt** done at once – **to get on to** to contact

Comprehension Questions

1. Why is the customer impressed?
2. What did the customers find when they opened the consignment?
3. How does the export manager explain the mistake?
4. Why is it important that the customer gets the rest of the cutlery as soon as possible?
5. What does the export manager propose the customer does with the 13 sets of *Arabesque* cutlery? Why does he suggest this?

14. What's in a number?

Customer: Metcalfe Motors Ltd., Collie speaking.

Manufacturer: Good morning, Mr Collie. This is Ian Best of Chalmers Ltd. I have here your order for 5 drills of the type HX 7000, marked 'urgent'.

Customer: Yes, we need the machines for a new plant which we are opening in September.

Manufacturer: Well, I'm afraid we can't promise delivery of them for six months – that'll make it December at the earliest.

Customer: December? Oh dear, that's a blow. Is there no way of pushing our order through before then? It really is very urgent.

Manufacturer: I'm afraid not. We've had such a great demand over the last few months and the shortage of skilled staff has been so acute, that we're faced with a huge backlog of orders. And of course, having to close down completely for a week during the steel-workers' strike didn't help matters.

Customer: Yes, I understand your position. But the fact remains we must have the machines for the 1st September. I'll have to think the situation over and look into the alternatives before I can make any decision. I'll ring you back later today or tomorrow.

Manufacturer: What I could suggest is that you order the HX 8000, – you've probably read about it in our catalogue.

Customer: The HX 8000? No, I don't think I have.

Manufacturer: It's our latest model in the HX series, and is basically an improved version of the HX 7000 – same size and range, but superior design and improved performance. It's quieter, too.

Customer: And when would be the earliest delivery date?

Manufacturer: If we gave your order priority, we could let you have them by the end of August.

Customer: That sounds hopeful. Could you let us have more detailed information about it and a quotation for five, then?

Manufacturer: Certainly. Or even better, our sales representative in your area, Mr Henshaw, can come and see you, then he can answer any questions you may have at the same time.

Customer: Fine. When can I expect him?

Manufacturer: I'll get him to phone you and make an appointment.

Customer: Good. I'll expect to hear from him shortly then. Thank you. Good-bye.

Annotations

drill instrument for making holes in hard substances – **acute** [ə'kju:t] great, serious – **huge** [hju:dʒ] very great – **backlog** ['– –] accumulated business which has not yet been attended to – **to look into** to investigate

Comprehension Questions

1. Why is Metcalfe Motors' order urgent?
2. What is the delivery time for the drills? Why is it so long?
3. What is the customer's reaction to this news?
4. What alternative does the manufacturer suggest?
5. What is the HX 8000? How does it compare with the HX 7000?
6. When can Chalmers Ltd. deliver the HX 8000?
7. What does the customer ask for? What does the manufacturer suggest instead?
8. What do you think of Mr Best as a salesman?

33

15. An angry customer

Manager: Morgan here.

Customer (annoyed): This is Bryce speaking, of Southend Insurance. I'm ringing about the dictating machines we ordered from you three months ago.

Manager: Oh yes, I remember.

Customer: I'm glad about that. We thought you'd forgotten. We were promised delivery for June 15th, when we moved to our new offices. It's now July 28th, and not only have we not received the dictating machines, but nobody at your end seems to know anything about them.

Manager: I'm very sorry about the delay, Mr Bryce, but due to illness and holidays we've been very short-staffed recently.

Customer: Five weeks ago I was told there had been a mix-up with the order, but everything was sorted out. Then I was told there had been a hold-up in the factory, because of a shortage of parts. Now you tell me you're short-staffed.

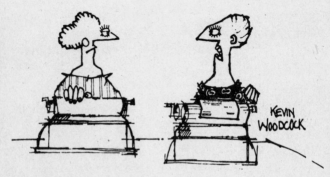

"My typxwritxr's gonx wring."

Manager: I'm really very sorry, Mr Bryce, but these things are quite beyond our control.

Customer: That's as may be, but this isn't the first time you've let us down. At the same time as the dictating machines we also ordered six electric typewriters.

Manager: Yes, I believe they were delivered on time.

Customer: Well, three days late, in fact.

Manager: Oh dear.

Customer: And when they did arrive, two had the wrong keyboards and one didn't work.

Manager: I take it these have now been replaced.

Customer: Yes, but we had to wait three weeks, which means that for three weeks three secretaries had to make do with old manual machines.

Manager: I'm very sorry about that – I'll look into the matter at once.

Customer: Yes, do so by all means, but it's a bit late now. What concerns me more at the moment is the dictating machines.

Manager: I'm pleased to say they are ready and awaiting shipment. You should receive them within the next three or four days.

Customer: Good. But if they're not here by next Monday – that is August 3rd – you can take the order as cancelled, and we'll order from another firm.

Manager: I'm sure that won't be necessary, Mr Bryce. I'll see to it myself that the machines go out today.

Customer: Well that's something, anyway.

Manager: And please accept my apologies for the inconvenience you've been caused. I assure you that such mix-ups are very rare with us.

Customer: I hope so. Well, I look forward to receiving the dictating machines within the next few days, then. Good-bye.

Annotations

mix-up ['– –] confusion involving mistakes – **hold-up** delay – **keyboard** ['kiːbɔːd] rows of keys on a typewriter – **to make do with s.th.** to manage with s.th. although it is not really satisfactory – **to look into s.th.** to investigate s.th. – **by all means** certainly – **to take s.th. as (cancelled)** to regard s.th. as (cancelled)

Comprehension Questions

1. Why is Mr Bryce so angry?
2. What excuse does Mr Morgan give for the delay?
3. What excuses was Mr Bryce given before?
4. How has Southend Insurance already been let down by Mr Morgan's firm?
5. What inconvenience did this previous let-down cause?
6. When can Mr Bryce expect to receive the dictating machines?
7. What does Mr Bryce threaten to do if the dictating machines don't arrive by August 3rd?

16. A matter of 10%

Secretary: Burrows Imports Ltd. Can I help you?

Exporter: Can I speak to Mr Turner, please?

Secretary: Who shall I say is calling?

Exporter: Herr Krieger of Wolters und Zwilling, Bremerhaven.

Secretary: Just a minute, Herr Krieger ...

Importer: Turner. Good morning, Herr Krieger.

Exporter: Good morning, Mr Turner. I'm phoning about your order for 150 *Dictamax* dictating machines and 100 *Addita* calculating machines, to be delivered by July 31st.

Importer: Oh, what's the problem?

Exporter: The problem is that you've based your order on the quotation we sent you last September. Since then we've had to put up all our prices by 10%.

Importer: Really? I didn't know that.

Exporter: Well, we sent a circular to all our customers informing them of the increase – perhaps you never received yours.

Importer: I certainly don't remember seeing anything about it, but I can check the correspondence files and see. 10% you say. That makes quite a difference.

Exporter: Yes, it's unfortunate that you didn't realize in time and order before the new prices were introduced. However, as you're a regular customer, we're prepared to offer you a 5% discount on this order, over and above your normal discount.

Importer: That puts things in a better light.

Exporter: On condition, that is, that you confirm the order with the new prices within two weeks – we'll send you a new price list today.

Importer: Right. We'll do that then. Can delivery still be made by the end of July?

Exporter: Yes – if we receive confirmation of the order within a fortnight, that should be no trouble.

Importer: Good. Well, thank you very much, Herr Krieger. I'm sorry about this mix-up.

Exporter: That's quite all right, Mr Turner. I'm glad we've managed to sort it out satisfactorily. Good-bye.

Annotations

circular ['sə:kjulə] a printed letter or announcement of which copies are made and distributed – **over and above** in addition to – **mix-up** ['– –] confusion involving mistakes – **to sort s.th. out** to find a solution for s.th.

Comprehension Questions

1. What have Burrows Imports Ltd. ordered?
2. What is wrong with the order?
3. Why should Burrows Imports Ltd. have known about the change?
4. What does Herr Krieger offer to do? Why does he make this offer?
5. On what condition is this offer made?
6. What effect will this delay have on the delivery date?

17. A complete write-off

An importer phones an exporter to inform him of a damaged consignment.

Importer: I'm phoning about the consignment of *Star Track* radio/cassette recorders, order number 59236, which arrived this morning. One case has been badly damaged by sea water and all the radios in it are a complete write-off.

Exporter: Oh, that's a nuisance. Have the surveyors seen it?

Importer: Not yet. We've been in touch with the Lloyd's surveyor here, and he's going to look into it this afternoon. We'll send you his report as soon as we have it. It was a c.i.f. shipment, so you've got the insurance policy there.

Exporter: Yes, we'll take the matter up with the insurers at once. Our policy covers us against all risks, so we're all right.

Importer: Are you covered for partial damage, too, as in this case?

Exporter: Yes. This sort of thing happens far too often for us to have an F.P.A. policy, as we found out to our cost before. So now we're always insured "with average".

"Be rather interesting to know if our insurance covers us against this sort of thing!"

Importer: That's just as well. The question now is when we can expect replacements.

Exporter: We can have another case ready at the docks by Wednesday, which means it can be dispatched on the *Southern Queen* sailing on that day. Arrival is due on the 29th of this month.

Importer: That'll be fine.

Exporter: By the way, what was the cause of the damage? Do you know?

Importer: It looks as if the hold was water-logged, but we'll have to wait for the surveyor's report to know for certain.

Annotations

write-off s.th. that has no value – **surveyor** [səˈveiə] person who examines the condition of buildings, cargo etc. – **partial** [ˈpɑːʃəl] not complete – **F.P.A.** Free of Particular Average: partial loss of cargo is not covered – **Particular Average/With Average** cargo is covered against partial loss – **hold** part of a ship where the cargo is stored – **water-logged** full of water

Comprehension Questions

1. What consignment is the importer ringing up about? What has happened to it?
2. What action has the importer already taken?
3. What is the importer going to send the exporter?
4. What action is the exporter going to take? Why?
5. What does the insurance policy cover the exporters against?
6. What sort of policy did they have before? Why did they change this?
7. What is the exporter going to do about replacing the damaged goods?

18. Hotel reservation

Receptionist: Dartington Hotel. Can I help you?

Secretary: This is Braun und Beier, Heidelberg. I'd like to reserve a single room with bath for four nights from 3rd September.

Receptionist: Just a minute please ... yes, that'll be all right. In whose name, please?

Secretary: Herr Roland Bartsch. He'll be arriving at Birmingham airport at 16.35. Could you arrange for him to be met?

Receptionist: Yes, of course.

Secretary: He'll also need a car for the duration of his stay. Could you arrange for one to be hired?

Receptionist: Yes, we can do that. With chauffeur?

Secretary: No, self-drive. And another thing, Herr Bartsch will be visiting the Toy Fair and will be meeting several business contacts. Has your hotel a conference room available for business meetings?

Receptionist: Yes, it has, but it's already booked for almost the whole of that week. The only time it's free during Herr Bartsch's stay is the afternoon of the 5th September from 2 o'clock onwards.

Secretary: Would you reserve it for him for that afternoon, then?

Receptionist: Yes, certainly. Will Herr Bartsch require an interpreter for the whole or a part of his visit?

Secretary: No, that won't be necessary. He speaks fluent English. Could you tell me your accommodation charge, so that I can estimate the expenses?

Receptionist: A single room with bath is £8 a day, plus a service charge of 12% and 11% VAT. This includes breakfast but not, of course, lunch or dinner.

Secretary: Could you send written confirmation of the reservation, please?

Receptionist: Yes, of course. And we'll look forward to welcoming Herr Bartsch. Good-bye.

Annotations

duration time during which something lasts – **VAT** value-added tax

Comprehension Questions

1. What does Herr Bartsch's secretary wish to reserve?
2. What other arrangements does she ask the hotel to make?
3. What is the purpose of Herr Bartsch's visit to Birmingham?
4. Why does the secretary ask whether the hotel has a conference room?
5. When is it free during Herr Bartsch's stay?
6. Why doesn't Herr Bartsch need an interpreter?
7. What does the hotel charge for a single room with bath? What is included in this price and what is not?
8. What does the secretary ask the receptionist to send her?

19. At the hotel at last

Herr Bartsch arrives at Birmingham airport, expecting to be met by someone from his hotel, but nobody appears. He waits for a while, and then takes a taxi. When he arrives at the hotel he is, naturally, quite annoyed.

Herr Bartsch: Good afternoon. My name's Bartsch. I've a room reserved here for four nights.

Receptionist: Oh, Herr Bartsch! You were supposed to be met at the airport, weren't you?

Herr Bartsch: Yes, I was. What happened?

Receptionist: I'm terribly sorry, Herr Bartsch. The car that was sent to meet you was involved in an accident on the way to the airport. We phoned the airport to let you know as soon as we heard, but you must have already left.

Herr Bartsch: I see. Well, it can't be helped.

Receptionist: I hope you didn't have any trouble finding the hotel.

Herr Bartsch: No, I took a taxi.

Receptionist: Yes, that's always the best idea in a strange city. And now if you'll write your name and address in the register here and sign it, the porter will show you your room. You're in room number 306 on the third floor.

Herr Bartsch: I hope it's quiet – there's a lot of noise in here from the traffic outside.

Receptionist: Oh yes, it's very quiet. It's at the back of the house where there's almost no traffic at all.

Herr Bartsch: That's good.

Receptionist: Dinner's served between seven and ten. The dining-room is through there.

Herr Bartsch: Ah yes, I see. And what about breakfast?

Receptionist: Breakfast is from seven to nine thirty. Do you wish to be called in the morning?

Herr Bartsch: Yes please – at six thirty.

Receptionist: And would you like early morning tea or papers?

Herr Bartsch: No tea, thank you, but I'd like the *Guardian* and the *Financial Times*.

Receptionist: Right – you can collect them from here tomorrow morning. And now, if you go with the porter he'll show you your room.

Comprehension Questions

1. Where does Herr Bartsch land?
2. How does Herr Bartsch get to his hotel?
3. Why is he annoyed when he arrives?
4. What explanation does the receptionist give?
5. What must Herr Bartsch do before being shown to his room?
6. What is Herr Bartsch worried about regarding his room? Why?
7. When does Herr Bartsch want to be called in the morning?
8. What else does he want in the morning? What doesn't he want?

20. Representation in Britain

At the Birmingham Toy Fair Herr Bartsch meets Mr Healey, a selling agent, whose firm is keen to represent Herr Bartsch's firm, Braun und Beier, in Britain. They meet at Herr Bartsch's hotel to discuss the details.

Herr Bartsch: From what I've heard, Mr Healey, your organization seems to be fairly well established. Could you tell me more about it?

Mr Healey: We're based in Birmingham, as you know, but we have offices in all the major cities, and in addition we have 15 regional offices covering the smaller towns and country areas.

Herr Bartsch: It sounds as if we'd be fully represented, then.

Mr Healey: Oh yes, you need have no fear in that direction.

Herr Bartsch: As you can understand, we can't afford not to be, with the competition there is today.

Mr Healey: Yes, of course. I take it you'd be granting us the sole agency.

"I thought putting your pin there might possibly have more results, Smedly!"

Herr Bartsch: Yes, we would. The contract would be for three years, after which it would be renewed annually.

Mr Healey: That would be all right. Would sales be on a consignment basis or by our placing firm orders?

Herr Bartsch: On consignment. We propose to give you 6 months' credit for the first consignment to give you a chance to launch our product on the market, and after that payment should be made quarterly, by draft.

Mr Healey: That's reasonable. We can't expect a very high turnover in the first six months.

Herr Bartsch: Exactly. As regards commission, we'll pay you 4 % on all sales, plus reasonable expenses. Do you agree?

Mr Healey: That sounds satisfactory. And what about advertising? Would you like us to take charge of that?

Herr Bartsch: Yes, it would be better. It would save us the bother and cost of translating and shipping advertising material.

Mr Healey: Right. The other thing is, how soon could you let us have the first supplies? It's less than 4 months to Christmas and we want to make the most of the seasonal trade.

Herr Bartsch: Yes, of course. I'll have a word with our order department and see that your orders are given priority.

Mr Healey: Thank you. Well, I think that's all.

Herr Bartsch: Right. I'll draw up a draft contract, then, and have it ready tomorrow afternoon. And now, how about dinner?

Annotations

bother trouble – **draft contract** Vertragsentwurf

Comprehension Questions

1. Who is Mr Healey? What are Mr Healey and Herr Bartsch meeting to discuss?
2. Why is Herr Bartsch satisfied that his firm would be fully represented by Mr Healey's firm?
3. Why is it important to Herr Bartsch that his firm is fully represented?
4. What sort of agency will Mr Healey's firm be granted by Braun und Beier? How long will the contract be for? What will happen after that?
5. On what basis are sales to be made?
6. How often must the account be settled? How is payment to be made?
7. What rate of commission will Mr Healey's firm be paid?
8. Who will see to the advertising? Why does Herr Bartsch think this arrangement would be best?
9. Why does Mr Healey want the first supplies as soon as possible?
10. What is Herr Bartsch going to do by the next afternoon?

21. A job well done

Mr Healey, a selling agent, talks to Mr Cox, a buyer.

Mr Cox: I hear you've been granted the sole agency for Braun und Beier toys. Is that right?

Mr Healey: Yes, we'd been hoping to get it for some time. Then I met their Export Manager at the Birmingham Toy Fair and we clinched the deal.

Mr Cox: My congratulations. You've done well there. Braun und Beier have a reputation for high quality, and they're supposed to be a pleasant firm to work with, too.

Mr Healey: Yes, they certainly made that impression.

Mr Cox: It's come at the right time of year too – just before Christmas.

Mr Healey: Yes, it's a great opportunity. It means a lot of work, though. It takes a great deal of organisation to launch a product onto the market successfully, and we haven't got much time. We've got all the advertising to see to, too, and there's a lot of competition at this time of year.

Mr Cox: You've certainly got a lot on your plate. Still, you'll be able to relax again once the Christmas rush is over.

Mr Healey: Not a bit of it. Our contract with Nilssen's is due for renewal, and if we're not careful we're liable to lose it.

Mr Cox: Oh? Why's that?

Mr Healey: We've had several differences of opinion over the past year, and the turnover has dropped considerably. One main factor was their rise in prices and bad delivery, but they put the blame on our selling methods.

Mr Cox: Is there any competition for the agency?

Mr Healey: Yes, there is, but we're preparing a detailed analysis of the trouble of the past year, together with positive suggestions for improvement. We'll try and come to a compromise on selling methods, too, although we don't see eye to eye on that subject.

Mr Cox: Well, I wish you the best of luck.

Mr Healey: Thank you. I've a feeling we're going to need it!

Annotations

to clinch to make or settle finally – **to relax** to take things easy, to rest – **not a bit of it** not at all – **to see eye to eye** to agree

Comprehension Questions

1. What does Mr Cox congratulate Mr Healey on?
2. What does Mr Cox say about Braun und Beier?
3. Why is acquiring the agency now going to mean a lot of work for Mr Healey?
4. Why won't Mr Healey be able to relax after Christmas?
5. What has caused the bad atmosphere between Mr Healey's firm and Nilssen's?
6. What action is Mr Healey's firm taking to try to keep the agency?

22. An agent in Italy

After receiving the quarterly report and statement from
their representative in Milan, the export manageress of a
fabric manufacturer's phones him up.

Sr Martinelli: Martinelli.

Mrs Cartwright: Good morning, Sr Martinelli. This is
Jean Cartwright of Western Fabrics. We've just
received your last statement and report – thank you,
by the way, for sending them so punctually and in such
detail.

Sr Martinelli: I like to keep things up to date.

Mrs Cartwright: And you've certainly done a great job in
establishing our products on the Italian market. The
turnover's increased by leaps and bounds since you
took over the agency. Congratulations.

Sr Martinelli: Thank you. I must admit it's been hard work
at times. Competition's very stiff at the moment.

Mrs Cartwright: Yes. That's why we were particularly
concerned to receive your report of complaints about
the consignment we sent you in June. You say that
two customers claim the fabric was stained.

Sr Martinelli: Yes, it was – I've examined the goods myself.
In each case there was extensive brown staining –
4 bales are completely unsaleable. I've since had two
more complaints, but I haven't had a chance to
investigate these yet.

Mrs Cartwright: How do you think this could have
happened?

Sr Martinelli: The fabric probably got wet, possibly in
storage.

Mrs Cartwright: I'll phone the warehouse afterwards and
get them to look into it.

Sr Martinelli: What about replacements? As you can imagine, the customers are very annoyed about the matter and it's important for future business that the material is replaced as soon as possible.

Mrs Cartwright: Yes, of course. I've already arranged for the replacements you asked for in your report to be sent by air. As soon as you let me know the extent of the damage in these other two cases, I'll have the necessary replacements sent for these, too.

Sr Martinelli: Good. I'll contact you when I have more details, then.

Mrs Cartwright: Thank you, Sr Martinelli. Good-bye.

Annotations

fabric ['– –] *here:* woven cloth – **by leaps and bounds** very rapidly – **stiff** *here:* great, hard – **bale** package of merchandise wrapped up in canvas – **to look into** to investigate

Comprehension Questions

1. Why does Mrs Cartwright congratulate Sr Martinelli?
2. Why are Western Fabrics particularly concerned about Sr Martinelli's reports of complaints from customers?
3. What have the customers complained about?
4. How does Sr Martinelli think the damage was caused?
5. What action is Mrs Cartwright going to take to find out the cause of the damage?
6. Why is it important for future business that the customers receive replacements for the damaged goods as soon as possible?
7. What arrangements has Mrs Cartwright made to have the goods replaced?

23. An expensive expense account

M Belloir: Belloir.

Mrs Cartwright: Good morning, Monsieur Belloir. Jean Cartwright of Western Fabrics here.

M Belloir: Ah, good morning, Mrs Cartwright. What can I do for you?

Mrs Cartwright: I've just been looking at your expense account of the last six months.

M Belloir: Oh yes? Is something not in order?

Mrs Cartwright: Well, as you know, in addition to your commission we agreed to pay any reasonable expenses.

M Belloir: Yes, that's right.

Mrs Cartwright: Well, I'm sure you'll understand that whereas we accept the occasional business lunch as necessary and beneficial, expensive meals for up to six people, almost daily, is stretching a point rather.

M Belloir: But the best way to get anything sold is over good food, as the increased turnover over the last few months shows.

Mrs Cartwright: Of course, but our profit margin is not so wide that we can afford this type of selling on such a large scale. Nor are we prepared to pay for cigars or large drink bills – apart from the odd exception, of course.

M Belloir: But you must appreciate that generous entertainment can often tip the balance when it comes to the decision whether or not to order.

Mrs Cartwright: Yes, but the amount of entertaining is quite out of proportion to the number of orders actually won.

M Belloir: But I am doing no more than anyone else in the business here. And with the stiff competition we've got at the moment, we can't afford to be mean.

Mrs Cartwright: Well, I'm sure we can rely on your discretion.

M Belloir: Of course.

Mrs Cartwright: But I'm afraid I must ask you to be a bit less extravagant, otherwise we shall be forced to set a limit on your account.

M Belloir: I see.

Mrs Cartwright: Well, that's all, then. I look forward to receiving your next report. Good-bye, Monsieur Belloir.

Annotations

beneficial [ˌbeni'fiʃəl] helpful, having good effect – **to stretch a point** to go beyond what is acceptable – **to tip the balance** to make (a decision) go one way or the other – **stiff** *here:* hard, difficult – **mean** ungenerous – **discretion** [dis'kreʃən] freedom to judge what is right or best – **extravagant** [iks'trævigənt]

Comprehension Questions

1. What is Mrs Cartwright phoning M Belloir about?
2. What payment had M Belloir been promised?
3. What does Mrs Cartwright object to about M Belloir's expense account?
4. What arguments does M Belloir put forward to justify it?
5. Why does Mrs Cartwright not accept these arguments?
6. What warning does Mrs Cartwright give M Belloir?

24. An invitation

Richard Saville: Richard Saville speaking.

Peter van Dyck: Hello, Richard, this is Peter van Dyck. I'm just ringing to let you know about a conference we're holding in Amsterdam next month to discuss European sales. It'll last three days, from 4th–6th May. Will you be able to come?

Richard Saville: 4th–6th you say? Yes, I can make that.

Peter van Dyck: Good. I'll send you a copy of the agenda, so you can be well-prepared.

Richard Saville: Thanks. I'm glad we're getting together again at last. Looking at the latest sales figures, we've got a lot to talk about. We'll have to take drastic action if we're not to lose our position on the European market to our competitors.

Peter van Dyck: Yes, that's why this conference has been called at such short notice. Do you know when you'll be coming? The conference starts at 9 a.m. on the 4th.

Richard Saville: In that case I'll fly over to Amsterdam the evening before.

Peter van Dyck: Well, let me know when you've made definite arrangements, and I'll arrange hotel accommodation for you, and for you to be met at the airport.

Richard Saville: Thank you. I'll give you a ring.

Peter van Dyck: By the way, could Margaret come over with you? There's a dinner and dance on the Friday evening for the conference participants and their husbands and wives.

Richard Saville: I'm sure she'd be pleased to come.

Peter van Dyck: And perhaps you'd both like to come and spend the weekend with us in Alkmaar afterwards.

Richard Saville: That sounds a lovely idea. Thank you very much.

Peter van Dyck: Good. I'll look forward to seeing you both in a couple of weeks then.

Annotations

participant [pɑːˈtisipənt] s.o. who takes part in s.th.

Comprehension Questions

1. What is Peter van Dyck phoning for?
2. Why is the conference being held?
3. What is Peter van Dyck going to send Mr Saville?
4. Why does Mr Saville think a conference on European sales is necessary?
5. When does Mr Saville intend flying to Holland?
6. What arrangements will Peter van Dyck make when he knows Mr Saville's time of arrival?
7. Why does Peter van Dyck ask Mr Saville if his wife could come too?
8. What does Peter van Dyck invite Mr Saville and his wife to do afterwards?

25. A job in England

Angelika Lenz wants to work in England for a while, so when she sees an advertisement for a 'secretary with fluent French and German', she applies and is invited for an interview.

Manager: Good afternoon, Miss Lenz. Please sit down.
Miss Lenz: Thank you.
Manager: I've studied your application form and curriculum vitae, but there are still a few questions I'd like to ask.
Miss Lenz: Yes, of course.
Manager: I see you left school at 18 with your school leaving certificate, and then you worked for a year in Paris, and after that with a firm in Manchester for a year. What did your duties there include?
Miss Lenz: At first I did mostly typing and translating – letters, prospectuses, telexes and so on – as well as general office work, of course. But in both cases I was also handling quite a bit of the routine German correspondence by the end of the year.
Manager: And then you went back to Germany, where you did a two-year course at a language school. You seem to have had quite a wide curriculum.
Miss Lenz: Yes, we did. Apart from English and French language we also had courses in commercial correspondence in English, French and German, typing and shorthand in all three languages, translations of commercial, political and economic texts, business law and import/export procedure.
Manager: It was certainly a comprehensive syllabus. And your exam results were very good, too. Then you worked for two years as a secretary with an engineering firm in Geislingen.

Miss Lenz: Yes, it was a small firm, and as I was the only person there with any knowledge of English, I was responsible for all communication with English and French-speaking countries, as well as having my normal secretarial duties.

Manager: It sounds like a good job. Why did you leave it?

Miss Lenz: Mainly because I wanted to work abroad for a time. Also, after two years the job was getting boring. I thought working for a larger company might be more interesting.

Manager: Well, I don't think you'd find time to be bored here. Apart from the correspondence, you'd also be required to arrange and attend business meetings – occasionally, but not often, in the evenings –, to be on the firm's stand at international exhibitions, and to accompany me on business trips to European countries abroad. It might mean packing your bags and leaving at quite short notice. Would you be prepared for such work?

Miss Lenz: Yes, if the rewards were high. What would my salary be?

Manager: You'd begin on £2,500 a year, plus luncheon vouchers, and of course overtime and expenses on such trips as I mentioned. You'd also get three weeks a year paid holiday.

Miss Lenz: It certainly sounds like the sort of job I had in mind.

Manager: And it sounds as if you'd be suited for it. Your English is excellent, and I see from your form that you have a shorthand speed of 100 words per minute and a typing speed of 40 words per minute – that's certainly up to standard. Miss Lenz, if you want the job, it's yours!

Annotations

comprehensive [ˌkɔmpriˈhensiv] including a lot – **syllabus** [ˈsiləbəs] programme of school studies

Comprehension Questions

1. What did Miss Lenz's jobs in Paris and Manchester involve?
2. What subjects did the syllabus at the language school include?
3. Where did Miss Lenz work when she finished at the language school? What did her job there involve?
4. Why did she leave her job?
5. What would be required of her if she took the secretarial position she is being interviewed for?
6. What would Miss Lenz be paid? What holiday would she get?
7. What are Miss Lenz's typing and shorthand speeds? Are these good?
8. Is Miss Lenz interested in the job? How do you know?

Suggested Answers
to the Comprehension Questions

1. Final arrangements

1. He is phoning up to discuss the arrangements for the course that some of his people are attending in Croydon.
2. The group will be arriving at Heathrow at 4.49 on Tuesday evening, May 14th.
3. Single rooms with baths have been reserved for them at the George Hotel in Croydon.
4. They will be flying back the evening that the course finishes. They are booked on the 20.45 flight from Heathrow.
5. He asks whether the people who are taking part in the course have received the information sheets which they sent out last week.
6. He says that it looks the most interesting course that they have had yet.

2. Mixing business with pleasure

1. Herr Hansen is the export manager of a German firm. Mr Evans is the manager of a large English car manufacturing firm.
2. They are meeting to discuss a device to reduce air pollution by cars which has been developed by Herr Hansen's firm and which Herr Hansen hopes to sell to Mr Evan's firm.
3. He says eating is an expensive business anywhere in London these days.

4. It will reduce pollution by cars by up to 70 per cent.
5. Because an American firm, *Cleanfilter*, recently produced a similar device. Herr Hansen thinks there is no danger because although *Cleanfilter's* device is similar in so far as it performs the same function, there are quite basic differences.
6. The German device has the advantage of being considerably cheaper than the American one. This is because of lower production costs and the lower import charges within the Common Market.

3. At an exhibition stand

1. They are dealers in office furniture and equipment.
2. She tells him that the cushions of the chair are fastened by a special tape and are changeable, and that the chair itself can be adjusted.
3. Because office workers spend so great a part of the day sitting down.
4. He likes the colour scheme, and the fact that there is sufficient drawer space for papers, files etc. He finds it unusual because it is not often you see such cheerful colours in an office.
5. It has been so designed that everything one needs can be kept within easy reach.
6. He intends to study the catalogue over lunch and come back sometime during the afternoon to place his order.

4. Life on strike

1. Because his wife has done nothing but complain all day.
2. Because by striking the electricity workers are helping the country on its way to economic ruin, instead of building it up.

3. He says that the electricity workers were promised a year ago that their pay situation would be reviewed annually to keep pace with inflationary trends, and as that promise has not been kept, they must fight for it.
4. Half the factories in the Midlands have been forced to stop production, and 20,000 men have been sent home. Ford claim that the strike has already wiped out their profit for the whole of this year.
5. Frank is pleased – he says it shows that they are having an effect, and they must stand firm.
6. No progress is being made at all, as neither the Union nor the employers will give an inch.

5. To smoke or not to smoke

1. It hopes to make the public aware that cigarette smoking harms the health.
2. It has sent out over two million leaflets, it has had posters printed and it has acquired free advertising space in many papers and magazines, as well as on radio and television.
3. Because the British Cancer Society held a similar campaign last year which didn't do the industry any harm.
4. They put a warning on cigarette packets, they no longer advertise on television and they contribute to Cancer Research.
5. The aim of the British Cancer Society is to make people aware that cigarette smoking harms the health, and to discourage people from smoking. The aim of the tobacco companies is to encourage people to smoke so that they will buy more and more cigarettes.

6. The missing money

1. It says that Mr Finney's account was overdrawn. He thinks it can't be true because he has kept a strict record of his expenses, and he should have £212.
2. According to the bank's records, nothing has been paid into his account for the last three months, and he has an overdraft of £128.
3. Because his firm assures him that his salary has been paid in every month as usual.
4. Because the bank changed over to a computer system three months ago, and there have been a few teething troubles.
5. He thinks that a slight error must have been made in programming.

7. Computerised Export Intelligence

1. He read their advertisement in the *Financial Times*.
2. Because smaller firms have not the facilities for market research that larger firms have.
3. It gets its information from its Commercial Diplomatic posts in many countries abroad.
4. It offers a wide selection of information, for example, notification of the changes in tariff and import regulations overseas, and information on potential markets.
5. The subscription is £25. This covers the service, the literature and the postage.

8. Starting up in Brazil

1. No, it is not. It has got competition from a French firm and an Italian one.
2. Because they have been trying to get into South America for a long time.
3. It is going to investigate the possibility of setting up a factory in Brazil.
4. They are encouraging foreign investment of all kinds, and there are practically no restrictions.
5. It looks healthy and it is expanding at an astonishing rate.

9. A new idea in shirts

1. Ten thousand men took part.
2. Because women usually have quite a bit of influence on what is worn by their husbands.
3. Most of the women said they thought they were a good idea.
4. 10 per cent would want to wear them themselves. The consultant said the others were mistrustful – Englishmen are on the whole very conservative about their clothes and not easily won over to new ideas and materials.
5. He advises the firm to aim their advertising at the businessman who has to travel and attend meetings, and the wife of such a man.

10. The wonders of the computer

1. He says they are unavoidably inaccurate and slow.
2. They are usually wrongly programmed.
3. All the facts about the stores situation, the customers'

names, addresses, reference numbers and details of
their accounts would be stored there.
4. When the facts changed the computer would automatically change its records.
5. At regular intervals you can have a printout of anything you want.
6. Because although the initial outlay is high, what you
save in labour costs and gain in efficiency would make
it worthwhile.

11. A change of plan

1. He is ringing about his order for spare parts for the
Cleanomat 460 washing-machines.
2. He wants the parts sent by air instead of by rail and
sea. This is because in the meantime the spares shortage
has become acute and they need the parts urgently.
3. He was paying by banker's transfer. The exporter now
wants him to pay by telegraphic transfer.
4. They are going to send them to the importer by airmail
as soon as they have confirmation from their bank that
they have received the importer's transfer.
5. He wants to pay for future orders by Documentary
Letter of Credit to be drawn at 60 days sight. The
exporter asks him to instruct his bank to open an
Irrevocable Letter of Credit in their favour through
Lloyds Bank, Portsmouth, for the amount on the
invoice.

12. A rush order

1. He is phoning from Hamburg.
2. He wants 1000 *Masterform* shirts to be sent to him as
soon as possible.

3. Because there has been a rush on them and they are almost out of stock.
4. It will be shipped c.i.f. Hamburg.
5. He also inquires about the winter catalogue and samples.
6. Mr Moore says that they have had a dispute in their dispatch department, which has held everything up.
7. The dispute has been settled and Herr Peters should be getting the catalogue and samples by the end of the week.

13. A wrong order

1. He is impressed because the order was delivered so promptly.
2. They found that they had received the wrong order.
3. He explains that they have several temporary workers in the packing department at the moment to enable them to cope with the Christmas rush.
4. Because he needs it for the Christmas trade.
5. He proposes that the customer keeps it if he is granted a 10% discount, as this would be easier than sending them back, and it would save the freight and insurance costs.

14. What's in a number?

1. Because they need the machines for a new plant which they are opening in September.
2. The delivery time is six months. It is so long because Chalmers Ltd. have had such a great demand over the last few months and they have been so short of skilled staff that they are faced with a huge backlog of orders.

3. The customer wants to think the situation over and look into the alternatives before making a decision.
4. The manufacturer suggests that he orders another model – the HX 8000.
5. The HX 8000 is the latest model in the HX series. It is the same size and has the same range as the HX 7000, but it is a superior design, has improved performance and is quieter.
6. They can deliver it by the end of August.
7. He asks for a quotation for five machines. The manufacturer suggests a visit from their sales representative in the area.

15. An angry customer

1. Because he has not received the dictating machines which were due for delivery almost two weeks ago.
2. He says they have been short-staffed recently due to illness and holidays.
3. First he was told there had been a mix-up with the order, then he was told there had been a hold-up in the factory, because of a shortage of parts.
4. Six electric typewriters which Southend Insurance ordered were delivered three days late, and two of them had the wrong keyboards and one didn't work. Then they had to wait three weeks for them to be replaced.
5. It meant that for three weeks three secretaries had to make do with old manual machines.
6. He can expect to receive them within the next three or four days.
7. He threatens to cancel the order and order from another firm.

16. A matter of 10 %

1. They have ordered 150 *Dictamax* dictating machines and 100 *Addita* calculating machines.
2. It is based on the quotation Burrows Imports Ltd. were sent last September, and since then Wolters und Zwilling have put up all their prices by 10 %.
3. Because Wolters und Zwilling sent a circular to all their customers informing them of the increase.
4. He offers to grant Burrows Imports Ltd. a 5 % discount on this order, over and above their normal discount. He makes this offer because they are regular customers.
5. It is made on condition that Burrows Imports Ltd. confirm the order with the new prices within two weeks.
6. It will have no effect on the delivery date as long as confirmation of the order is received within a fortnight.

17. A complete write-off

1. He is ringing up about a consignment of *Star Track* radio/cassette recorders. One case has been badly damaged by sea water and all the radios in it are a complete write-off.
2. He has been in touch with the Lloyd's surveyor.
3. He is going to send him the surveyor's report.
4. He is going to take up the matter with the insurers because, as it was a c.i.f. shipment, he has got the insurance policy.
5. It covers them against all risks.
6. They used to have an F.P.A. policy. They changed it because they often received partial damage which an F.P.A. policy did not cover them for.
7. He is going to have another case ready at the docks by Wednesday.

18. Hotel reservation

1. She wishes to reserve a single room with bath for four nights from 3rd September.
2. She asks them to arrange for Herr Bartsch to be met at the airport and for a self-drive car to be hired for the duration of his stay.
3. He is visiting the Toy Fair.
4. Because Herr Bartsch will be meeting several business contacts and will need somewhere for business meetings.
5. It is free on the afternoon of 5th September from 2 o'clock onwards.
6. Because he speaks fluent English.
7. It charges £8 a day, plus a service charge of 12% and 11% VAT. Breakfast is included in the price, but not lunch or dinner.
8. She asks her to send her written confirmation of the reservation.

19. At the hotel at last

1. He lands at Birmingham airport.
2. He takes a taxi.
3. Because nobody came to meet him at the airport.
4. She says the car that was sent to meet him was involved in an accident on the way to the airport.
5. He must write his name and address in the register and sign it.
6. He is worried about whether or not his room will be quiet because there is a lot of noise in the hotel from the traffic outside.
7. He wants to be called at six thirty.
8. He also wants two newspapers – the *Guardian* and the *Financial Times*. He doesn't want any tea.

20. Representation in Britain

1. Mr Healey is a selling agent. His firm is keen to represent Herr Bartsch's firm in Britain, and he and Herr Bartsch are meeting to discuss details.
2. Because Mr Healey's firm has offices in all the major cities in Britain, plus 15 regional offices covering the smaller towns and country areas.
3. They can't afford not to be fully represented because of the competition from other firms.
4. It will be granted the sole agency. The contract will be for three years. After that it will be renewed annually.
5. Sales are to be made on a consignment basis.
6. The account must be settled quarterly. Payment is to be made by draft.
7. It will be paid 4 % commission on all sales.
8. Mr Healey's firm will take charge of the advertising. Herr Bartsch thinks this arrangement would be best because it would save his firm the bother and cost of translating and shipping advertising material.
9. Because it is less than four months to Christmas and he wants to make the most of the seasonal trade.
10. He is going to draw up a draft contract.

21. A job well done

1. He congratulates him on having been granted the sole agency for Braun und Beier toys.
2. He says they have a reputation for high quality and that they are supposed to be a pleasant firm to work with.
3. Because it takes a great deal of organisation to launch a product onto the market successfully, and they have not got much time until Christmas. They have also got all the advertising to see to, and there is a lot of competition at this time of year.

4. Because their contract with Nilssen's is due for renewal and they are in danger of losing it.
5. They have had several differences of opinion over the past year, and the turnover has dropped considerably. Mr Healey's firm thinks this is due to Nilssen's rise in prices and bad delivery, but Nilssen's put the blame on Mr Healey's firm's selling methods.
6. They are preparing a detailed analysis of the trouble of the past year, together with positive suggestions for improvement. They will also try and come to a compromise on selling methods.

22. An agent in Italy

1. Because the turnover of Western Fabrics' products has increased by leaps and bounds since he took over the agency.
2. Because competition is very stiff at the moment.
3. They have complained that the fabric was stained.
4. He thinks the fabric got wet, possibly in storage.
5. She is going to phone the warehouse and get them to look into it.
6. Because the customers are very annoyed about the matter.
7. She has arranged for the replacements Sr Martinelli asked for in his report to be sent by air.

23. An expensive expense account

1. She is phoning him about his expense account.
2. He had been promised his commission plus any reasonable expenses.
3. He has been doing too much extravagant entertaining.

4. He says that the best way to get anything sold is over good food, as the increased turnover over the last few months shows, and that generous entertainment can often tip the balance when it comes to a decision whether or not to order.
5. Mrs Cartwright says that their profit margin is not so wide that they can afford that type of selling, and anyway the amount of entertaining is quite out of proportion to the number of orders actually won.
6. She warns him that unless he is a bit less extravagant they will be forced to set a limit on his account.

24. An invitation

1. He is phoning to let Richard Saville know about a conference that is being held in Amsterdam next month.
2. It is being held to discuss European sales.
3. He is going to send him a copy of the agenda.
4. He thinks that looking at the latest sales figures, they have got a lot to talk about. If they don't take drastic action they will lose their position on the European market to their competitors.
5. He intends flying on the evening of the 3rd May.
6. He will arrange hotel accommodation for him and for him to be met at the airport.
7. Because there is a dinner and dance on the Friday evening for the conference participants and their husbands and wives.
8. He invites them to spend the weekend with him and his wife in Alkmaar.

25. A job in England

1. They involved typing, translating letters, prospectuses, telexes and so on, general office work, and later handling the routine German correspondence.
2. It included English and French language, commercial correspondence, typing and shorthand in all three languages, translations of commercial, political and economic texts, business law and import/export procedure.
3. She worked with an engineering firm in Geislingen. Her job there involved all communication with English and French-speaking countries plus normal secretarial duties.
4. Because she wanted to work abroad for a time. Also the job was getting boring, and she thought working for a larger company might be more interesting.
5. She would be required to handle correspondence, arrange and attend business meetings, be on the firm's stand at international exhibitions and to accompany her boss on business trips to European countries abroad.
6. She would be paid £2,500 a year, plus luncheon vouchers, and overtime and expenses on trips. She would get three weeks a year paid holiday.
7. She has a typing speed of 40 words per minute and a shorthand speed of 100 words per minute. Yes, these are good.
8. Yes, Miss Lenz is interested in the job. She says: "It certainly sounds like the sort of job I had in mind."

Phrases

On the telephone

This is Mr Jones speaking, of Thompson Welders Ltd.
Jones am Apparat, von der Firma Thompson Welders Ltd.

Richard Jenkins here.
Hier ist Richard Jenkins.

John North Ltd. Can I help you?
John North Ltd. Was kann ich für Sie tun?

This is the Richmond Insurance Company.
Hier ist die Richmond Versicherung.

Can I/May I speak to Monsieur Belloir?
Kann ich bitte Monsieur Belloir sprechen?

Would you put me through to the export department, please?
Würden Sie mich bitte mit der Exportabteilung verbinden?

I want to speak to someone about our account.
Ich möchte jemanden wegen unseres Kontos sprechen.

Please would you connect me with the personnel department?
Würden Sie mich bitte mit der Personalabteilung verbinden?

Who's speaking, please?
Wer ist am Apparat, bitte?

Who shall I say is calling?
Wen darf ich melden?

Could you give me your name, please?
Darf ich um Ihren Namen bitten?

I'm afraid Mr Bell is out/still at lunch/not in the office/not available/at a meeting.
Herr Bell ist leider nicht da/noch zu Tisch/nicht im Büro/nicht zu sprechen/in einer Besprechung.

Shall I ask him to call you back?
Soll ich ihn bitten, Sie zurückzurufen?

Can you ring again in about an hour/later?
Können Sie in etwa einer Stunde/später wieder anrufen?

Should he contact you?
Soll er sich mit Ihnen in Verbindung setzen?

Can I take a message?
Kann ich etwas ausrichten?

Can you give me your name and telephone number?	Wie ist bitte Ihr Name und Ihre Telefonnummer?
His number's engaged. Do you want to wait?	Er telefoniert gerade. Möchten Sie warten?
I'll put you through.	Ich verbinde.
I'll ring back.	Ich rufe zurück.
I'm afraid I've got the wrong number.	Ich fürchte, ich bin falsch verbunden.
Hold the line, please.	Bleiben Sie bitte am Apparat.
I'm afraid there's no answer on number 6 57 94.	Apparat 6 57 94 meldet sich nicht.
Could you speak louder/ more clearly, please?	Könnten Sie bitter lauter/deutlicher sprechen?
Could you spell that, please?	Könnten Sie das bitte buchstabieren?
Good-bye.	Auf Wiederhören.

Inquiries

I'm calling in answer to your advertisement in the *Sunday Times*.	Ich rufe wegen Ihrer Anzeige in der *Sunday Times* an.
Your name was given to us by a business friend.	Wir erhielten Ihren Namen von einem Geschäftsfreund.
We've been referred to you by Morgan Evans Ltd.	Sie wurden uns durch die Firma Morgan Evans Ltd. empfohlen.
We saw your stand at the Frankfurt Book Fair.	Wir haben Ihren Stand auf der Frankfurter Buchmesse gesehen.
I believe you manufacture measuring instruments.	Ich glaube, Sie stellen Meßinstrumente her.
We are interested in importing Japanese cameras into Germany.	Wir sind daran interessiert, japanische Photoapparate nach Deutschland zu importieren.
I understand you are one of the largest manufacturers of filters in Europe.	Wie ich höre, sind Sie einer der größten Filterhersteller Europas.

We are retailers/importers/ wholesalers in the fur trade.	Wir sind Einzelhändler/Importeure/Großhändler in der Rauchwarenbranche.
We've had several inquiries from our customers for tweed fabrics.	Wir haben seitens unserer Kunden mehrere Anfragen nach Tweedstoffen gehabt.
There's a promising market here for pocket calculators.	Hier ist ein vielversprechender Markt für Taschenrechner.
Could you please send us your catalogue/price list?	Könnten Sie uns bitte Ihren Katalog/Ihre Preisliste schicken?
Could you send us samples of your winter fabrics?	Könnten Sie uns einige Proben/Muster Ihrer Winterstoffe schicken?
Could you give us a quotation for/quote us for ten HX 8000 drills?	Könnten Sie uns ein Angebot machen für zehn HX 8000 Bohrer?
We would like to place a trial order.	Wir möchten einen Probeauftrag erteilen.
The prices you quoted are far too high.	Die Preise in Ihrem Angebot sind viel zu hoch.
If you'll reduce your prices by 5 per cent, we'll place an order for 2000.	Wenn Sie Ihre Preise um 5 % nachlassen, erteilen wir einen Auftrag über 2000 Stück.
Do you think you could arrange a visit from your representative/ a demonstration?	Könnten Sie bitte veranlassen, daß Ihr Vertreter uns aufsucht/ eine Vorführung stattfindet?
When can we expect delivery?	Wann können wir mit der Lieferung rechnen?
What's the earliest date you can deliver?	Welches ist Ihr frühester Liefertermin?
If you can guarantee delivery of the goods within three weeks ...	Wenn Sie uns die Lieferung der Waren innerhalb von drei Wochen garantieren können ...
What are your terms of delivery/payment?	Was sind Ihre Liefer-/Zahlungsbedingungen?

We can supply excellent references.

Wir können ausgezeichnete Referenzen nennen.

Morgan Evans Ltd. will give you any information you wish to know about us.

Die Firma Morgan Evans Ltd. wird Ihnen alle gewünschten Auskünfte über uns geben.

Quotations and offers

We can deliver straight from stock.

Wir können sofort ab Lager liefern.

We've got a delivery time of three weeks for these models.

Wir haben drei Wochen Lieferzeit für diese Modelle.

We can deliver the goods as soon as we receive your order.

Wir können die Waren liefern, sobald wir Ihre Bestellung erhalten.

We'll dispatch them tomorrow c.i.f. Hamburg.

Wir werden sie morgen cif Hamburg verschicken.

You'll find the machines you inquired about on pages 74 to 79 in our catalogue.

Sie finden die Maschinen, nach denen Sie sich erkundigt haben, auf den Seiten 74 bis 79 unseres Katalogs.

On page 16 of our catalogue you'll see our latest range of office furniture.

Auf Seite 16 unseres Katalogs finden Sie unser neuestes Büromöbelangebot.

These models can be had with a number of variations.

Diese Modelle sind mit verschiedenen Variationen zu haben.

We recommend article no. 2106 as being of a particularly high quality.

Wir empfehlen den Artikel Nr. 2106 als qualitativ besonders gut.

We grant a trade discount of 20 % on our list prices.

Wir gewähren einen Händlerrabatt von 20 % auf unsere Listenpreise.

Our catalogue prices are subject to a special discount of 5 %.

Auf unsere Katalogpreise gewähren wir einen Sonderrabatt von 5 %.

Our prices are quoted f.o.b. London/duty unpaid.

Unsere Preise verstehen sich fob London/unverzollt.

The quantity discounts mentioned in our price list vary according to the size of the order.

Die in unserer Preisliste angegebenen Mengenrabatte richten sich nach der Größe der Bestellung.

Due to rising costs we've had to increase our prices by 8 %.

Wegen steigender Kosten mußten wir unsere Preise um 8 % erhöhen.

As you're a regular customer we're prepared to offer you a 5 % discount.

Da Sie ein Stammkunde sind, sind wir bereit, Ihnen einen Rabatt von 5 % zu gewähren.

We can let you have a special discount of 3 % on your first order.

Auf Ihren ersten Auftrag können wir Ihnen einen Sonderrabatt von 3 % gewähren.

For a quantity of 100 or more we can allow you a special discount of 15 % on the prices quoted.

Bei einer Menge von 100 oder mehr können wir Ihnen auf die genannten Preise einen Sonder-rabatt von 15 % einräumen.

Our terms of payment are:
cash in advance
cash with order (c.w.o.)
cash on delivery (c.o.d.)
payment monthly/quarterly/on sight.

Unsere Zahlungsbedingungen:
Vorauskasse
Kasse bei Auftragserteilung
gegen Nachnahme
Zahlung monatlich/quartals-weise/bei Sicht.

We can arrange open account terms for you on receipt of the usual references.

Bei Vorlage der üblichen Referenzen können wir Ihnen offenes Ziel gewähren.

We expect settlement quarterly by Bill of Exchange or Banker's Draft.

Zahlung erfolgt vierteljährlich per Wechsel oder Banktratte.

Our terms for first orders are payment in advance or cash against documents (c.a.d.).

Unsere Konditionen für erste Bestellungen sind Vorauszahlung oder Kasse gegen Dokumente.

We can allow you three month's credit for future orders.

Für zukünftige Bestellungen können wir Ihnen 90 Tage Ziel gewähren.

As our prices are so favourable, our terms of payment are 30 days net.

Da unsere Preise so günstig sind, erfolgt Zahlung innerhalb 30 Tagen ohne Abzug.

Orders

We're almost out of stock of *Masterform* shirts. Can you let us have 1000 more as soon as possible?

Unser Lagerbestand an *Masterform* Hemden geht zu Ende. Können Sie uns so bald wie möglich noch 1000 Stück senden?

Could you enter the following order for immediate delivery.

Würden Sie bitte folgenden Auftrag zur sofortigen Lieferung vormerken.

Please, would you send us 600 desk calenders and charge them to our account.

Würden Sie uns bitte 600 Schreibtischkalender schicken und unser Konto damit belasten.

It's important that we receive the goods by 31st January.

Es ist wichtig, daß wir die Waren bis zum 31. Januar erhalten.

If the goods are not delivered by that date, then we'll have to cancel the order.

Wenn die Lieferung nicht bis zu dem Termin erfolgt, sehen wir uns gezwungen, die Bestellung zurückzuziehen.

Would you please confirm this order.

Würden Sie diesen Auftrag bitte bestätigen.

If any of the items are out of stock, could you give us a quotation for a substitute.

Bitte senden Sie uns für nicht-vorrätige Artikel ein Ersatz-angebot.

Your order is already being carried out and it will be delivered in accordance with your instructions.

Ihr Auftrag wird bereits ausge-führt, die Lieferung erfolgt laut Ihren Anweisungen.

Our forwarding agents will collect the consignment next week, and let you have all details regarding delivery.

Unsere Spedition wird die Sen-dung nächste Woche abholen und Ihnen alle Einzelheiten über die Lieferung mitteilen.

I'm afraid the cloth you ordered is out of stock/ no longer available.	Der von Ihnen bestellte Stoff ist leider nicht vorrätig/nicht mehr lieferbar.
We no longer stock these articles.	Diese Artikel führen wir nicht mehr.
We can offer you a substitute which is the same price and of similar quality (to the fabric you ordered).	Wir können Ihnen zum selben Preis einen Ersatz von ähnlicher Qualität (wie der bestellte Stoff) anbieten.

Packing and dispatch

We'll dispatch the goods tomorrow c.i.f. Hamburg.	Wir werden die Waren morgen cif Hamburg versenden.
If we can get them on the *Tilbury Star,* sailing on Wednesday, they'll arrive in Hamburg on the 28th.	Wenn wir sie auf der *Tilbury Star* verschiffen können, die am Mittwoch ausläuft, werden sie am 28. in Hamburg eintreffen.
How do you want the goods sent, by sea or air?	Sollen die Waren per Schiff oder Luftfracht versandt werden?
We can have the cases at the docks ready for shipment on Wednesday.	Wir können die Kisten am Mittwoch versandfertig im Hafen haben.
Your order is ready and awaiting shipment.	Ihr Auftrag ist ausgeführt und versandbereit.
Would you please be sure to observe our packing instructions.	Bitte beachten Sie unbedingt unsere Verpackungshinweise.
Please pack the goods in strong wooden cases with waterproof lining.	Bitte verpacken Sie die Waren in stabilen Holzkisten mit wasserdichter Auskleidung.
Would you please make sure the goods sent exactly match the description on the invoice, to avoid delay at customs.	Bitte sorgen Sie dafür, daß die versandten Waren mit der Beschreibung auf der Rechnung genau übereinstimmen, um eine Verzögerung beim Zoll zu vermeiden.

As well as the Commercial Invoice we require a Consular Invoice and Certificate of Origin.

Neben der Handelsrechnung benötigen wir Konsulatsfaktura und Ursprungszeugnis.

The shipping documents have been sent to the Mercantile Bank Inc., New York, with a sight draft for $7,000.

Die Versandpapiere/Verschiffungsdokumente sind zusammen mit einer Sichttratte über $7000 an die Mercantile Bank, Inc., New York, geschickt worden.

The shipping documents will be sent to you by our forwarders.

Die Versandpapiere werden Ihnen von unserem Spediteur zugeschickt.

The consignment scheduled to arrive here on March 14th still hasn't arrived.

Die Sendung, die am 14. März hier hätte eintreffen sollen, ist noch nicht angekommen.

Four bags were missing from the consignment delivered to us on 14th June. Would you please look into this matter immediately.

Aus der Sendung, die uns am 14. Juni geliefert wurde, fehlten vier Säcke. Wir bitten Sie, die Angelegenheit umgehend zu prüfen.

Accounts and payment

What conditions must we fulfil to have open account terms?

Unter welchen Bedingungen können Sie uns offenes Ziel gewähren?

How do you wish payment to be made?

Wie soll die Zahlung erfolgen?

We'll arrange for our bank to issue a banker's transfer/telegraphic transfer.

Wir werden durch unsere Bank eine Banküberweisung/telegraphische Überweisung vornehmen lassen.

We would suggest paying for future orders by Documentary Letter of Credit/Irrevocable Letter of Credit.

Wir schlagen vor, daß die Zahlung für künftige Aufträge per Dokumenten-Akkreditiv/unwiderrufliches Akkreditiv erfolgt.

Would you instruct your bank to open an Irrevocable Letter of Credit in our favour for the amount on the invoice?	Bitte eröffnen Sie durch Ihre Bank über den Rechnungsbetrag ein unwiderrufliches Akkreditiv zu unseren Gunsten.
Payment's being made by banker's draft in settlement of your invoice for $400.	Zahlung erfolgt per Banktratte zum Ausgleich Ihrer Rechnung über $400.
We've opened a Letter of Credit with the Union Bank.	Wir haben bei der Union Bank ein Akkreditiv eröffnet.
Please draw $400 on us at 90 days sight.	Bitte ziehen Sie auf uns $400 per 90 Tage Sicht.
We can't let you have any more credit until your account has been paid.	Wir können Ihnen keinen Kredit mehr einräumen bis Ihr Konto ausgeglichen ist.
Your payment has been overdue since 10th May.	Ihre Zahlung ist seit dem 10. Mai fällig.
It is no doubt an oversight on your part.	Sie haben es zweifellos übersehen.
We must insist on receiving payment by 30th June. Failing this we shall be compelled to take legal action.	Wir müssen darauf bestehen, daß die Zahlung bis zum 30. Juni erfolgt. Andernfalls sind wir gezwungen, gerichtliche Schritte einzuleiten.
Would you allow me to postpone settlement of our account.	Würden Sie mir einen Zahlungsaufschub gewähren?
We suggest making part payment of £200 now and paying the balance by September 20th.	Wir schlagen eine sofortige Teilzahlung von £200 vor und Begleichung der Restsumme bis zum 20. September.
As you've always paid promptly in the past, we're prepared to allow you to postpone payment now.	Da Sie bisher immer rechtzeitig gezahlt haben, sind wir bereit, Ihnen jetzt einen Zahlungsaufschub zu gewähren.
I'm afraid we cant't allow you to postpone payment.	Leider können wir Ihnen keinen Zahlungsaufschub gewähren.

Since our profit is marginal, we cannot make exceptions to our terms of payment.

Da unser Gewinn gering ist, können wir bei unseren Zahlungsbedingungen keine Ausnahmen machen.

Your failure to pay on time is in turn causing us financial embarrassment.

Ihre Nichtzahlung zum vereinbarten Termin bringt uns auch in finanzielle Schwierigkeiten.

The remainder must be paid in monthly instalments.

Die Restsumme muß in monatlichen Raten gezahlt werden.

Complaints

We've received the wrong order.

Wir erhielten die falsche Bestellung.

We've still not received the dictating machines we ordered on May 21st.

Wir haben die Diktiergeräte, die wir am 21. Mai bestellten, immer noch nicht erhalten.

We were promised delivery for June 28th.

Die Lieferung wurde uns zum 28. Juni zugesagt.

If you don't deliver the goods by July 31st we'll have to order from another firm.

Wenn Sie die Waren nicht bis zum 31. Juli liefern, sind wir gezwungen, sie bei einer anderen Firma zu bestellen.

If the goods are not here by next Monday, August 3rd, we shall have no alternative than to cancel the order.

Wenn die Waren bis nächsten Montag, den 3. August, nicht hier sind, sehen wir uns gezwungen, den Auftrag zurückzuziehen.

15 of the last consignment of radios are a complete write-off.

Aus der letzten Sendung Radios müssen 15 völlig abgeschrieben werden.

One case has been badly damaged by sea water.

Eine Kiste ist durch Meerwasser stark beschädigt worden.

Five of the typewriters don't work.

Fünf der Schreibmaschinen funktionieren nicht.

How soon can we expect replacements?	Wann können wir mit Ersatz rechnen?
It's important that we have them as soon as possible.	Es ist wichtig, daß wir sie so bald wie möglich erhalten.
We're prepared to keep the goods if you allow us a reduction of 10 %.	Wir sind bereit, die Waren zu behalten, wenn Sie uns einen Preisnachlaß von 10 % gewähren.
This has caused us a great deal of inconvenience.	Dies hat uns große Ungelegenheiten bereitet.

Replies to complaints

We'll send you a new consignment/replacements immediately.	Wir schicken Ihnen sofort eine neue Sendung/Ersatz.
Could you return the goods so that we can inspect them?	Könnten Sie uns die Waren zur Begutachtung zurückschicken?
I'm very sorry about the delay.	Für die Verzögerung bitte ich um Entschuldigung.
It was due to a hold-up in the factory/a shortage of parts.	Es wurde verursacht durch eine Verzögerung in der Fabrik/ einen Mangel an Ersatzteilen.
We've been very short-staffed recently, due to illness and holidays.	In letzter Zeit hatten wir wegen Krankheit und Urlaub wenig Personal.
I'm afraid there was a mix-up with the order.	Leider wurde Ihr Auftrag fehlgeleitet.
I'll look into the matter at once.	Ich werde die Angelegenheit sofort prüfen.
Your order's being dealt with now.	Ihr Auftrag wird jetzt bearbeitet.
You should receive the replacements within the next few days.	Innerhalb der nächsten Tage müßte Ersatz bei Ihnen eintreffen.

We've had such a great demand over the last few months that we're faced with a huge backlog of orders.	Wir hatten in den letzten Monaten eine so große Nachfrage, daß wir einer großen Anzahl unerledigter Aufträge gegenüberstehen.
Having to close down during the steelworkers' strike didn't help matters.	Daß wir während des Streiks der Stahlarbeiter schließen mußten, hat die Sache noch verschlimmert.
I'll get on to our dispatch department at once.	Ich werde mich sofort mit unserer Versandabteilung in Verbindung setzen.
I apologize for the mix-up.	Entschuldigen Sie bitte das Versehen.

Insurance

We would like the goods sent c.i.f. Rotterdam.	Bitte schicken Sie die Waren cif Rotterdam.
We suggest that we take out an open policy for £50,000 worth.	Wir schlagen eine offene Police (Generalpolice) über £50 000 vor.
The policy covers against all risks except war risk.	Die Police deckt alle Risiken, außer Kriegsrisiko.
We're covered for partial damage/"with average"/ F.P.A. (= Free of Particular Average).	Wir sind versichert gegen Teilschaden/mit (einschließlich) Havarie/frei von (ausschließlich) besonderer Havarie.
Part of the consignment we received this morning was damaged.	Ein Teil der Sendung, die wir heute morgen erhielten, war beschädigt.
The goods in one case are a complete write-off.	Die Waren in einer Kiste müssen völlig abgeschrieben werden.
We've been in contact with the Lloyd's surveyor.	Wir haben uns mit dem Sachverständigen von Lloyd's in Verbindung gesetzt.

We've arranged for the surveyor to investigate the extent of the damage.

Wir haben dafür gesorgt, daß das Ausmaß des Schadens durch den Sachverständigen festgestellt wird.

We'll send you the surveyor's report and our insurance claim as soon as possible.

Wir werden Ihnen den Bericht des Sachverständigen und unseren Versicherungsanspruch so bald wie möglich zuschicken.

We'll take the matter up with the insurers at once.

Wir werden die Angelegenheit sofort mit der Versicherung besprechen.

What was the cause of the damage?

Was hat den Schaden verursacht?

Travel arrangements

Hotel:

I wish to make a reservation.

Ich möchte … reservieren lassen.

Have you a double room free for the 28th October?

Haben Sie am 28. Oktober ein Doppelzimmer frei?

I'd like to reserve a single room with bath for four nights from 3rd September.

Ich möchte ab 3. September für vier Nächte ein Einzelzimmer mit Bad reservieren lassen.

Could you tell me how much you charge?

Können Sie mir Ihre Preise nennen?

Are service and VAT (value-added tax) included in the price?

Sind Bedienung und Mehrwertsteuer im Preis inbegriffen?

Do you require a deposit?

Ist eine Anzahlung erforderlich?

Do you have facilities for business meetings/ a conference room?

Haben Sie Räumlichkeiten für Geschäftsbesprechungen/ einen Sitzungssaal?

Could you arrange for a chauffeur-driven/self-drive car to be available on my arrival.

Könnten Sie dafür sorgen, daß mir bei meiner Ankunft ein Wagen (mit Chauffeur) zur Verfügung gestellt wird.

Where's the bar?

Wo ist die Bar?

Plane:

I'd like to book a flight to Geneva on April 24th.	Ich möchte für den 24. April einen Flug nach Genf buchen.
How much is the single/return fare?	Wieviel kostet ein einfacher Flug/ein Rückflugticket?
I wish to travel first/economy class.	Ich möchte erster Klasse/Touristenklasse fliegen.
What time does the plane leave/arrive?	Wann fliegt das Flugzeug ab/landet es?
When can I collect my tickets?	Wann kann ich meine Tickets abholen?
Can I reserve a seat?	Kann ich einen Platz reservieren lassen?
Can you arrange for a hired car to be at the airport for me on my arrival?	Können Sie bitte dafür sorgen, daß bei meiner Ankunft ein Mietwagen für mich am Flughafen bereitsteht?
I wish to make a reservation for the Dover to Calais car ferry/hovercraft on June 28th.	Bitte reservieren Sie mir für den 28. Juni einen Platz auf der Autofähre/dem Luftkissenfahrzeug von Dover nach Calais.

Agencies

We're looking for someone to represent us in Canada.	Wir suchen einen Vertreter für Kanada.
We want to sell our products in your country.	Wir wollen unsere Produkte in Ihrem Lande verkaufen.
The Chamber of Commerce recommended you as a possible agent for our products in Holland.	Die Handelskammer hat Sie als möglichen Agenten für unsere Produkte in Holland empfohlen.
We're looking for someone to take over our agency in Italy.	Wir suchen jemanden, der unsere Agentur in Italien übernimmt.

We hear you are now in a position to accept further agencies for the American market.	Wie wir hören, sind Sie nun in der Lage, weitere Vertretungen für den amerikanischen Markt zu übernehmen.
I understand that you're not represented in Switzerland.	Ich höre, daß Sie in der Schweiz nicht vertreten sind.
I hear you are looking for a reliable representative in Paris.	Ich habe gehört, daß Sie einen zuverlässigen Vertreter in Paris suchen.
It's important that we should be fully represented.	Es ist wichtig, daß wir auf breitester Basis vertreten werden.
We understand that you have good connections with department stores and specialist shops.	Wie wir hören, haben Sie gute Beziehungen zu Warenhäusern und Spezialgeschäften.
I've been selling furniture in France for the last ten years and have built up a number of reliable contacts.	Ich verkaufe seit zehn Jahren Möbel in Frankreich und habe einige zuverlässige Beziehungen aufgebaut.
We would be granting you the sole agency/you would be the sole agents.	Wir würden Ihnen die Allein-Vertretung überlassen.
The contract would be for three years, after which it would be renewed annually.	Es würde sich um einen Drei-jahresvertrag handeln, der nach Ablauf jährlich verlängert würde.
Sales are on a consignment basis/by placing firm orders.	Die Waren sind in Kommission/auf eigene Rechnung.
You'll be paid 4% commission on all sales.	Wir zahlen Ihnen 4% Provision auf alle Bestellungen.
Payment is to be made quarterly by draft.	Zahlung erfolgt vierteljährlich per Tratte.
We agree to pay reasonable expenses.	Wir sind bereit, angemessene Unkosten zu vergüten.
We'll accept the cost of the advertising.	Wir übernehmen die Werbe-kosten.

| We'll send you any advertising material you need. | Wir schicken Ihnen alle Werbe-materialien, die Sie brauchen. |
| I'll draw up a (draft) contract. | Ich werde einen Vertrag(sent-wurf) erstellen. |

Applying for a job

I saw your advertisement in last Sunday's *Observer* for an electrical engineer.	Ich habe Ihre Stellenanzeige 'Elektro-Ingenieur' im *Observer* vom letzten Sonntag gelesen.
I'm calling about the secretarial post you're advertising in today's *Times*.	Ich rufe wegen der Sekretärin-nen-Stelle an, die Sie in der heutigen *Times* annoncieren.
Mr Jones tells me that you're looking for an efficient salesman/a secretary with a good knowledge of German.	Herr Jones sagte mir, daß Sie einen tüchtigen Verkäufer/eine Sekretärin mit guten Deutschkenntnissen suchen.
I trained for three years as a welder.	Ich wurde drei Jahre als Schweißer ausgebildet.
I did my secretarial training at the language school in Bochum.	Ich habe meine Ausbildung zur Sekretärin an der Sprachen-schule in Bochum gemacht.
I served a three-year apprenticeship as a printer with Meier Ltd. in Mannheim.	Ich legte eine dreijährige Lehre als Drucker bei der Firma Meier GmbH in Mannheim ab.
I studied physics and chemistry at Stuttgart University.	Ich habe an der Universität Stuttgart Physik und Chemie studiert.
I have a shorthand speed of 100 words per minute and a typing speed of 40 words per minute.	Ich schreibe 100 Wörter pro Minute (= etwa 140 Silben) Kurzschrift und 40 Wörter pro Minute (= etwa 200 Anschläge) auf der Maschine.